Bolivia travel Guide 2024:

Discover Hidden Wonders: Insider Insights and Must-Visit Destinations for an Unforgettable Journey.

Christian David

All rights reserved. No part of this publication may be reproduced, distributed, or transmitted in any form or by any means, including photocopying, or other electronic or mechanical method, without the prior written permission of the publisher, except in the case of brief quotations embodied in critical reviews and certain other non commercial uses permitted by copyright law.

Copyright © Christian David, 2024.

Table of content

Chapter 1. Introduction   6
  Overview of Bolivia   6
  Purpose of the Travel Guide   8
  What's New in 2024   10

Chapter 2. Essential Travel Information   13
  Visa and Entry Requirements   13
  Currency and Banking   16
  Language and Communication   19

Chapter 3. Planning Your Trip   23
  Best Time to Visit   23
  Itinerary Suggestions   26
  Packing Tips and Essentials   29

Chapter 4. La Paz: The Capital City   34
  Exploring the Historic Center   34
  Cultural Attractions   37
  Bolivian Cuisine: A Culinary Journey   41

Chapter 5. Natural Wonders and Adventure Travel   45
  Salar de Uyuni   45
  Amazon Rainforest   49
  Lake Titicaca   52

Hiking and Trekking	56
Mountain Biking	60
Wildlife Encounters	65

Chapter 6. Indigenous Cultures and MustSee Destinations 69

Traditional Festivals	69
Local Markets	75
Interacting with Indigenous Communities	80
Sucre	85
Potosi	89
Rurrenabaque	93

Chapter 7. Hidden Gems and Bolivian Cuisine 98

OfftheBeatenPath Towns	98
Secret Natural Spots	102
Unique Experiences	106
Culinary Traditions	111
Signature Dishes	115
Local Markets and Street Food	119
Transportation Tips	128
Cultural Etiquette	132

Chapter 9. Photography Guide 138

Capturing Bolivia's Beauty	138
Best Photo Spots	142
Editing and Sharing Tips	146

Chapter 10. Conclusion 151
Recap of Highlights 151
Inspiring Future Travelers 154

Chapter 1. Introduction

Overview of Bolivia

Hello friends! Welcome to Bolivia, the land of vibrant colours, rich culture and beautiful landscapes. As we begin this journey together, let me share with you my personal thoughts on the fascinating profile of Bolivia. Located in the heart of South America, Bolivia fascinates with its rich culture and nature. From the highest peaks of the Andes to the lush jungles of the Amazon basin, Bolivia's diverse landscapes are a testament to its uniqueness.

As I walk the lively streets of La Paz, the world's highest capital, I am surrounded by the energy of its markets, the sounds of indigenous languages and the aromas of local food. Bolivia's cultural richness is woven into the fabric of everyday life, where ancient traditions coexist with modern rhythms. The Salar de Uyuni, the world's largest salt flat, unfolds like an otherworldly mirror, reflecting the vastness of the sky. Journeying through this surreal landscape is a humbling experience, connecting us to the raw beauty of nature. Venturing into the Amazon Rainforest, the air becomes thick with the sounds of exotic creatures, and every step unveils the secrets of this lush ecosystem. Bolivia's commitment to preserving its ecological treasures is evident, making it a haven for nature enthusiasts.

This travel guide is much more than a collection of facts; invites you to discover Bolivia's hidden treasures, taste its unique cuisine, dance in celebration, and connect with its passionate people. So buckle up and start an adventure in Bolivia, where each episode will reveal something new about this beautiful country. Let's go! Let's start our journey together.

Purpose of the Travel Guide

This travel guide is designed to be your compass for Bolivia's spectacular landscapes and vibrant culture. Whether you're an experienced hiker or a firsttime adventurer, this guide is designed to be your trusted companion and provide insight and advice that goes above and beyond.

Our aim is not only to give you information, but also to provide you with information. We want you to feel the heartbeat of Bolivia, taste its unique flavors and connect with its diversity. By entering the meaning of each place, we try to uncover the hidden treasures that make Bolivia the jewel in the heart of South America.

Practical and inspiring, this guide fuels your desire to travel while also providing essential travel tips. Whether you are looking for the joy of adventure in the wonders of Bolivia, its rich culture, or its delicious food, our goal is to take you on an unforgettable and unforgettable experience.

As you turn the pages of these pages, imagine yourself traveling to the bustling markets of La Paz, crossing the vast Salar de Uyuni and immersing yourself in Bolivian culture and indigenous communities. Let this guide be your gateway to an unforgettable trip to Bolivia, where we will uncover hidden gems and reveal the soul of this beautiful country.

What's New in 2024

As we enter 2024, Bolivia is ready to offer new experiences and exciting developments that will add another layer to its already impressive record. Here are the 2024 updates:

Environmental Initiatives: Bolivia is achieving a sustainable economy with new environmental initiatives. From conservation projects in the Amazon rainforest to ecoconscious accommodation, travelers can now enjoy the country's sense of responsibility.

Renaissance cuisine: Bolivian cuisine has undergone a renaissance by combining aromatic herbs with modern ingredients. Discover delicious cuisine in cities like La Paz, where innovative chefs combine local ingredients with international influences.

Digital Nomad Hotspot: Bolivia is becoming a digital nomad hotspot as remote workers seek inspiration. Find a coworking space in a beautiful location where you can work surrounded by Bolivia's beautiful scenery.

Festival Feasts: Bolivia's festivals are legendary and will reach new heights in 2024. Learn the power of traditional celebrations with modern challenges to make them more memorable.

Art and Culture Centers: Bolivian cities are turning into vibrant art and culture centers. Explore art districts, galleries and cultural centers that showcase the creativity and talent of local artists and offer a new perspective on Bolivia's cultural dominance.

CommunityBased Tourism: Partner with Bolivia's indigenous communities through communitybased tourism. These experiences provide authentic interactions that allow visitors to learn about and contribute to the country's rich cultural heritage.

Improve Infrastructure: Improve transportation and infrastructure to make it easier for travelers to explore various parts of Bolivia. From road improvements to connectivity, these improvements make travel easier and make traveling around the country easier.

When you go to Bolivia in 2024, expect a combination of culture and innovation, nature and technology to create a modern and timeless journey. Discover something new and let Bolivia's newest service enhance your exploration of this extraordinary place.

Chapter 2. Essential Travel Information

Visa and Entry Requirements

According to Bolivia's immigration policy, it is an important step in making it competitive and fun. Here is a detailed guide to 2024 visas and entries:

Tourist Visa: Most tourists to Bolivia, regardless of nationality, can enter the country for tourist purposes without a visa and stay for more than 90 days. Make sure your passport is valid for at least six months before you plan to travel.

Visa Extension: If you plan to stay longer than the initial 90 days, it is recommended that you visit the Bolivian Immigration Office for information on visa extension options.

Visas for Certain Nationalities: Nationals of certain countries may require a visa before arriving in Bolivia. Please check with your nearest Bolivian embassy or consulate for visa requirements specific to your country.

Yellow Fever Vaccination: Bolivia may require proof of vaccination against yellow fever if you are coming from or traveling through a country that is particularly at risk of yellow fever. Check the latest health requirements before travelling.

Entry points: Bolivia has several entry points, including major airports such as El Alto International Airport in La Paz and Viru Viru International Airport in Santa Cruz. Make sure the entry point you choose suits your travel plans.

Proof of onward travel: It is advisable to provide proof of onward travel, such as a return ticket, as immigration authorities may request documentation of this letter upon arrival.

Arrival Form: Prepare to complete Arrival Form Provide information about your stay in Bolivia upon arrival. These forms are usually distributed during your flight or when you arrive at the airport.

Border crossing: If you are entering Bolivia by land, please check the specific entry conditions for the border crossing you plan to use as these may vary. Please note that visas and immigration procedures are subject to change, so it is important to obtain the latest information from official sources or contact your nearest Bolivian consulate or embassy before travelling.

By making sure you meet all the necessary requirements, you can focus on enjoying the wonders Bolivia has to offer. Travel safe!

Currency and Banking

Understanding the currency and banking industry is essential to properly manage your finances when you travel to Bolivia. As of 2024, the country's currency and banking systems are as follows:

Currency: Bolivia's currency is the Bolivian Bolivia (BOB). Please learn about currency and exchange rates before arriving.

ATMs and Payments: ATMs are widely available in the city, and many accept major credit and debit cards. However, it is recommended that you carry some cash, especially when traveling to remote areas where card acceptance may be limited.

Currency Exchange: Currency exchange services are available at airports, banks and exchange offices throughout Bolivia. Compare exchange rates to make sure you're getting the best value for your money.

Credit and Debit Cards: Credit and Debit Cards are generally valid in city centers, hotels and supermarkets. Visa and Mastercard are widely used, while American Express and Diners Club are more widely accepted.

Passengers: Travelers' checks are not accepted in Bolivia and you may have problems trying to cash them. It is recommended that you use a combination of cash and cards to meet your financial needs.

Bank Hours: Banks in Bolivia are generally open Monday through Friday, with some branches offering limited service on Saturdays. Plan your financial transactions accordingly, especially if you need holiday banking services.

Foreign Exchange Fees: Be aware of foreign exchange fees and consider exchanging small amounts of currency in advance to pay fees promptly. Monitor exchange rates throughout your trip for many great currency exchange opportunities.

Hidden Fees: Beware of foreign exchange fees or ATM withdrawal fees when using your card abroad. Contact your bank before the tour to check their fee structure.

Safety Notes: Be careful when using ATMs, especially in crowded areas. Choose an ATM in a welllit and safe location, and be careful when handling money in public places.

By understanding the benefits of currency and business in Bolivia, you will be able to manage your finances well and enjoy a great trip. Always prioritize the security of your financial transactions and stay informed about changes in the local financial environment. Travel safe!

Language and Communication

Language is a common element that unites the diversity of Bolivian culture. Understanding the nuances of communication is not only essential, but also key to connecting with the heart of this fascinating country. As of 2024, the official languages and communications in Bolivia are:

Working Languages: Bolivia recognizes many languages, with Spanish as their first language word. Additionally, 36 Aboriginal languages are spoken, reflecting the cultural diversity of the country.

Spanish Basics: Although many Bolivians (especially those living in cities) speak Spanish, it helps to know some basic phrases. Politeness is important, so learning greetings, thank yous, and expressions can improve your conversations.

Main Languages: In some areas, particularly in rural areas and Aboriginal communities, people may speak Aboriginal languages. Learning a few words or phrases in the local language can improve connection and interest.

Language School: Consider taking a short language course or hiring a local tour guide who can help with translation. This not only enhances your travel experience but also supports the local community.

Nonverbal Communication: Nonverbal cues are very important in Bolivian communication. Pay attention to gestures, facial expressions, and body language as they often convey subtle meanings.

Cultural Sensitivity: Bolivia's cultural geography is diverse and some topics may be more sensitive than others. Be careful and thoughtful in your conversations, and ask for information about local customs to guide the conversation appropriately.

Tourist Areas: English can be widely spoken in tourist areas. But there is still value in knowing some Spanish to gain more experience and for situations where English is not widely understood.

Translation App: Provide mobile assistance with the Translation App. These can be important tools in overcoming language problems, especially when dealing with less common languages.

Patience and openness: Patience is a virtue in communication. Make time to learn and communicate, even if there are occasional language problems. Bolivians are often proud of their generosity in blending their language and culture.

By becoming familiar with Bolivia's many languages and communicating with an open mind, you will find this language to be your bridge to authentic experiences and meaningful connections during your travels. Thank you! (Good luck!)

Chapter 3. Planning Your Trip

Best Time to Visit

Choosing the best time to visit Bolivia is key to making the most of its diverse sights and festivals. The following tips can help you understand the season and find the best time to travel:

Season (MayOctober): This period is considered the dry season and the skies are clear and cool. hot. Now is the time to explore the Andes region, including popular destinations like La Paz and Salar de Uyuni. Dry air increases visibility and provides a great view for photography.

Rainy Season (November to April): The rainy season brings lush greenery, perfect for exploring the Amazon rainforest. However, this also means that the roads are difficult in some areas, so be prepared if you are going to a remote area. The Yongas region, known as the "Road of Death", is particularly affected by heavy rains.

Carnival season (FebruaryMarch): Bolivia's Carnival is a colorful celebration, dance and music, especially in Oruro. If you're interested in celebrating culture, plan your visit now. This is a time of strength and energy, but the need for help may be high.

Festivals and Events: Besides Carnival, Bolivia has many festivals throughout the year, each with a unique cultural experience. The Inti Raymi Festival in June celebrates the Inca sun god, while other events highlight Aboriginal traditions and legends. Check the festival calendar to match your visit with the festival.

Wildlife Watching: If wildlife watching is important, the dry season is generally better. During this period, animals in the Amazon rainforest are more active and the fresh air is suitable for bird watching and trips to explore different cultures.

Altitude Note: Bolivia's higher altitudes, including La Paz, can be cooler, especially at night. Be prepared for different weather conditions and pack appropriately, including warm layers.

OffPeak Travel (April and November): Consider traveling during the shoulder season between April and November to offset the clouds, the atmosphere is good for crowds. When the weather is bad you can still visit many places.

Plan by Event: Customize your visit to specific events. The dry season is a better choice for hiking and outdoor adventures, while those who love local culture and festivals may prefer to visit the festival during Carnival or other events.

Ultimately, the best time to visit Bolivia depends on your interests, the experiences you are looking for, and the areas you plan to explore. Whether you're interested in the highaltitude wonders of the Andes or the natural beauty of the Amazon, Bolivia has something to offer yearround.

Itinerary Suggestions

Make the most of your trip to Bolivia with comprehensive itineraries designed to provide a blend of culture, nature and unforgettable experiences. The following guide will take you to this beautiful country:

Itinerary 1: Andean Adventure

1-3. Days: La Paz

Explore the historical centre, Witches Market and Plaza Murillo. Take the cable car for a panoramic view of the city. Taste local cuisine in a traditional Bolivian restaurant.

4-6. Days: Salar de Uyuni

Take a scenic walk across the world's largest salt flat. Visit Inkawasi Island and its unique cactus forest. Witness the fascinating train cemetery of Uyuni.

7-9. Day:

Sucre Discover the colonial charm of the historic center of Sucre, a UNESCO World Heritage Site. Visit the Textile Museum and Freedom House. Hike to Maragua Crater for beautiful views.

Itinerary 2: Amazon Rainforest Exploration

1-3. Days: Rurrenabaque

Start your adventure at the door of the Amazon. Follow the guide in Madidi National Park and meet wild animals. Explore the pampas and learn about their many species and animals.

Days 4-6: Trinidad

Tour the rivers and lakes around Trinidad. Visit Aquaquana Preserve for bird watching and forest walks. Immerse yourself in Aboriginal culture and traditions.

7-9. Days: Riberalta

Head to Riberalta for the peaceful Amazon. Explore local shops and the beach. Participate in environmentally friendly activities and promote community tourism.

Itinerary 3: Culture and Gastronomy

1-3. Days: Cochabamba

Local cuisine at the Anticuchos Fair. Visit the iconic Christ the Redeemer statue. Explore business streets and squares.

4-6. Days: Potosi

Discover the history of the world's highest city. Visit the mines of Cerro Rico for a unique experience. Visit Casa Moneda and the Convent of Santa Teresa.

7-9. Days: Oruro

Immerse yourself in the rich culture of Oruro. Explore museums and art galleries. If possible, plan your visit during the busy Carnival season.

These tours provide insight into Bolivia's diverse landscapes and culture. Customize it to your liking and length of stay and prepare for an adventure that will leave you with lasting memories.

Packing Tips and Essentials

Smart packing is essential for a successful and enjoyable trip to Bolivia, where a variety of landscapes and cultures await you. Here are some packing tips and essentials for your adventure:

Clothing and Accessories:

Clothes to wear: The weather can change a lot in Bolivia. Wear layers for cooler nights and higher altitudes, and lighter clothing in hot climates.

Comfortable walking shoes: Whether you are walking in the city or in nature, comfortable and durable walking shoes are a must.

Raincoat: If you're visiting during the rainy season, bring a light, waterproof jacket and possibly a poncho in case of emergency downpours.

Day Protection: Bolivia's high altitude means more sunlight. Bring sunscreen, sunglasses and a widebrimmed hat for protection.

Bag: Small bag for daily travel that carries essential items like water, snacks and camera.

Health and Safety:

Altitude Sickness Medication: If you are traveling to a high altitude location like La Paz, consider bringing sickness or treatment medications with you.

Travel Insurance: Make sure you have travel insurance that covers medical and accident expenses.

Basic First Aid Kit: Prepare a first aid kit with basic supplies such as painkillers, bandages, and selfmedication.

Electronics and information:

Adapters and Chargers: Type A and Type C electrical outlets are commonly used in Bolivia. Bring adapters and chargers suitable for your device.

Photography Equipment: If you are a passionate photographer, do not forget to bring your camera, extra batteries and memory cards to capture the beautiful scenery of Bolivia.

Information: Bring your passport, visa (if required), travel insurance documents and a printout of your travel plan. Also consider using digital backup.

Other Items:

Reusable Water Bottle: It is important to stay hydrated, especially at high altitudes. Bring a reusable water bottle and refill it regularly.

Snacks: Bring energy bars or snacks for small meals, especially while walking.

Long Pillows and Blankets: For a long trip or plane ride, sleeping pillows and blankets can help you rest better.

Language Guide or App: A simple language guide or translation app can be useful, especially if you plan to go off the beaten path.

Be sure to customize your packaging to fit your specific needs and events. By packing the right things, you can focus on immersing yourself in the beauty and culture Bolivia has to offer. ¡Oh to Felizvia! (Have a good journey!)

Chapter 4. La Paz: The Capital City

Exploring the Historic Center

Exploring Bolivia's historic center is like entering a living museum, where exhibits, treasures and the pulse of local life interact. Below is a guide to the historic center of the Bolivian city, with a special focus on La Paz:

La Paz: Historical Tapestry

Plaza Murillo: Start your trip at Plaza Murillo in the heart of La Paz. This large city is surrounded by landmarks such as the Presidential Palace and the Cathedral of Our Lady of Peace. Witness the changing of the guard and increase the power.

Mercado de las Brujas: Step into the mysterious side of La Paz at Mercado de las Brujas. Look for shops stocking herbs, potions and traditional medicines. Don't miss the colorful show of amulets and llama fetuses believed to bring good luck.

San Francisco Church: Immerse yourself in the religious and architectural heritage of La Paz by visiting the San Francisco Church. Admire its baroque exterior and step inside to discover the ornate interior, which reflects a mix of Aboriginal and colonial influences.

Calle Jaén: Walk along Calle Jaén, a beautiful cobblestone street lined with wellkept buildings that are now museums. Explore the Musical Instrument Museum and the Gold Museum to understand Bolivia's culture and rich history.

Museo Nacional de Arte: Discover Bolivian art through the ages at the National Museum of Art. Housed in a beautifully restored building, the museum contains many paintings, sculptures and contemporary works that provide insight into the evolution of Bolivian art.

Museo de la Coca: Get a unique view of the cultural significance of the coca leaf at the Coca Museum. Learn about the traditional uses, rituals and controversies surrounding this plant.

Mirador Killi Killi: Visit Mirador Killi Killi for panoramic views of La Paz and its historical centre. This viewpoint allows you to enjoy stunning views of the city nestled among the mountains.

Gastronomic delights: End your exploration of the historical district with a meal of Bolivian cuisine at a local restaurant. Try salteñas (salted pastries), anticuchos (grilled skewers), or dishes featuring quinoa and Andean side dishes.

Exploring the historical sites of La Paz and other Bolivian cities is a journey through time, with every corner telling stories of the past and the beautiful culture of the present. Walk the cobblestone streets, mingle with the locals and let Bolivia's history unfold before you. ¡Buena Research! (Happy exploring!)

Cultural Attractions

Bolivia's culture is rich and diverse, blending indigenous culture, colonial influences, and modern expressions. Here's a guide to some of Bolivia's cultural attractions:

Tiahuanaco Archaeological Site: Explore the ancient ruins of Tiahuanaco, a UNESCO World Heritage Site near Lake Titicaca. Marvel at the originality of the stone carvings and discover the archaeological remains of an ancient civilization that flourished around 1500 BC.

Chiquitos Jesuit Mission: Visit the Chiquitos Jesuit Mission, a collection of wellpreserved churches showing a combination of indigenous and European architectural styles. These missions spread throughout the Chiquitania region and provide an insight into the history of Jesuit missionaries in Bolivia.

Tiahuanacu Museum: Immerse yourself in the history of the Tiahuanacu civilization at the Tiahuanacu Museum in La Paz. The museum's exhibits provide insight into the culture, art and technology of the ancient Andean civilization.

Museo Nacional de Etnografía y Folklore (National Museum of Ethnography and Folklore): Located in La Paz, this museum offers research on the diversity of Bolivia. From traditional clothing and artwork to presentations of Aboriginal rituals, it lets you learn about the country's rich traditions.

Tarabuco Market: Experience the beauty and diversity of Bolivia at Tarabuco Market. The local market near Sucre takes place every Sunday and is a gathering of locals displaying handicrafts, textiles and accessories.

Inti Raymi Festival: If you visit in June, don't miss the Inti Raymi Festival, a celebration of the Inca sun god. Featuring colorful parades, traditional dances and ceremonies, the festival opens a unique window into Bolivia's indigenous heritage.

Valle de la Luna (Valley of the Moon): Located just outside La Paz, Valle de la Luna is a surreal region formed by volcanic eruptions. Take a guided tour and learn about the geological history and cultural significance of this site.

Casa de la Moneda: In Potosi, discover the Casa de la Moneda, a historic mint that played an important role during the Spanish colonial period. The museum displays the machines used to mint coins and provides insight into the economic history of Bolivia.

Aboriginal Festivals: Various indigenous festivals are held throughout the year in Bolivia. These celebrations often include dances, music and rituals that reflect the traditions of different cultures.

Feast of Our Lady of Urcupinha: Celebrated in Cochabamba in August, this celebration honors Our Lady of Urcupinha and includes a performance of beauty, traditional dancing and powerful dress. It is an expression of religion and culture.

Whether exploring ancient sites, visiting indigenous markets or attending festivals, Bolivia's culture invites you to connect with the heart and soul of the country. The country is diverse and attractive. Entertainment! (Happy!)

Bolivian Cuisine: A Culinary Journey

Enter Bolivian cuisine, where the cuisine combines indigenous traditions, colonial influences, and a variety of ingredients. Here's your guide to the world of Bolivian food:

Salteñas: Begin your adventure with salteñas, delicious pastries filled with mouthwatering meat, vegetables and spices. These delicious dishes, mostly consumed as snacks, vary in composition and regional style.

Sopa de Mani (Peanut Soup): Among Bolivian soups, Sopa de Mani stands out. These peanut butter soups contain fruit and vegetable juices and often include chicken or beef. This is a comfort food favorite across the country.

Silpancho: Silpancho is a dish originating from Cochabamba that showcases breaded fried veal cutlets served with rice. It is a delicious and satisfying dish served with fried eggs, sliced tomatoes and onions.

Quinoabased dishes: Given Bolivia's Andean heritage, quinoa is a staple food. Try quinoa soup, salad, or a traditional quinoabased dish called risotto.

Camel and Alpaca Meat: Learn the difference between camel and alpaca meat. This meat can be grilled or boiled, giving it the flavor of Bolivia's highaltitude cooking tradition.

Anticuchos: Anticuchos are marinated and grilled skewers and are usually served with potatoes and spicy peanuts. This street's popular dishes combine ethnic and Spanish influences.

Humintas: Humintas are steamed tortillas filled with cheese and wrapped in corn husks. You can eat these delicious foods as a snack or side dish, especially during the holidays.

Bolivian Empanadas: Bolivian empanadas come in many varieties and include meat, cheese, and vegetables. These delicious pastries are a crowd pleaser and the perfect snack.

Chairo Soup: Originating from the Andean region, Chair soup is a hearty dish made from freezedried potatoes, vegetables and various meats. Its rich taste reflects Bolivia's diverse agricultural products.

Api: End your adventure with api, a hot drink made from bloody corn, spices and sugar. Often served with pastries or tamales, api is a popular beverage during holidays and cold weather.

Bolivian Wine: Explore Bolivia's extensive wine industry. The Tarija region is famous for its vineyards producing special highaltitude wines. Pair a local wine with your meal for a fun experience.

Cholitas Wrestling: While not a meal, the Cholitas Wrestling experience in La Paz provides entertainment and culture. Watch Aboriginal women wearing traditional clothing show off their skills and enjoy local snacks and fresh produce.

Bolivian cuisine is a blend of flavors and cultural influences. As you taste each dish, you'll discover the rich culinary traditions that make Bolivia the perfect destination for food lovers. Buen Procho! (Enjoy your meal!)

Chapter 5. Natural Wonders and Adventure Travel

Salar de Uyuni

Welcome to Salar de Uyuni, the world's largest salt flat, with endless white mountains reaching into view, creating a surreal and fascinating experience. Here are your clues to this mystery:

Salt Desert: Salar de Uyuni is located in western Bolivia and spans 10,000 square kilometers of dazzling salt crust. During the dry season, these vast lands resemble a continuous white desert, creating another place in the world.

Mirror effect: During the rainy season (November to March), a thin layer of water turns the salt into a giant face, forming the famous glass. . Reflections of the sky and clouds blur the horizon, making you feel like you're walking on clouds.

Incahuasi Island: Rising from the salt flats, Incahuasi Island, also known as Fish Island, is a rocky outcrop covered with cacti. Explore the island and enjoy panoramic views of the Salar and the surrounding landscape. The contrast between the green plants and the white expansion is striking.

Cactus Garden: Incahuasi Island has a beautiful Cactus Garden with towering cacti (some over 10 meters in height) in this special growing well. Walk in the footsteps of ancient giants and feel the peace around you.

Photography Paradise: Salar de Uyuni is a photographer's dream. The vast flat landscape and unique photographs make this a perfect place for imaginative and imaginative photography. Reflective surfaces and changes in light provide the last chance to capture stunning shots.

Stargazing: At night the Salar de Uyuni turns into the perfect place for stargazing. The highest point in the sky offers an uninterrupted view of the stars, providing an unforgettable stargazing experience.

Flora and Fauna: Despite its negative symptoms, Salar de Uyuni is not alive. During the rainy season, flamingos and other birds visit the shallow waters surrounding the salt flats. The contrast between the red flamingos and the white landscape is fascinating.

Uyuni Village: Use Uyuni Village as the entrance to the salt house. The city offers accommodation, guided tours, and the opportunity to learn more about the history and culture of the region.

Star Wars Wired: Some scenes from the movie Star Wars: The Last Jedi were shot on the Salar, which increases the request to fans of the series please.

Helpful Tips:

Altitude: Salar de Uyuni is at a higher altitude so it is easy to change.

Tour: Consider a tour to enjoy the uniqueness and safety measures of the salt flats.

SEASONAL VARIATIONS: Experiences vary seasonally, so choose the time of your visit based on your preferences. Salar de Uyuni is more than just a place; It is an art canvas that invites you to travel, wonder and immerse yourself in one of the most beautiful places in the world.

This is an adventure that will leave you with memories as big and lasting as the salt flats. ¡ Bienvenidos al Salar de Uyuni: You definitely have a Webtalk page! (Welcome to Salar de Uyuni!)

Amazon Rainforest

Dive into the lush embrace of the Bolivian Amazon Rainforest, where biodiversity thrives in one of the most biodiverse regions in the world. Here is your guide to discovering this wonder:

Pando Region: Start your Amazon adventure in Pando Region, where lush forests and flowing rivers offer an unforgettable experience. The city of Kobija is the gateway to this vast green land.

Madidi National Park: Explore the depths of the Amazon by visiting Madidi National Park, a UNESCO World Heritage protected area spanning a wide range of ecosystems. From lowland mountains to Andean cloud forests, Madidi is a haven for wildlife and nature lovers.

Stunning Biodiversity: Madidi is known for its extraordinary biodiversity with many species of animals and plants. Jaguars, tapirs and capybaras roam the jungle, while macaws and toucans fill the air with bright colors and music.

Indigenous communities: Meet the indigenous communities that call the Amazon home. Learn about their culture, sustainable lifestyle and deep connection with the forest. Participate in community tourism to promote and enjoy their rich heritage.

Water Adventure: Embark on an adventure on the river and travel the winding path through the forest. Explore a hidden backwater lake, spot dolphins and witness the beautiful dance of colorful butterflies along the river.

Eco Lodges and Treetop Cabins: Immerse yourself in the Amazon by staying in an Eco Lodge or Treetop Cabin. These services harmoniously combine comfort and ecological practice, offering you a unique opportunity to immerse yourself in the sights and sounds of the forest.

Birding Paradise: The Bolivian Amazon is a birding paradise. Home to over a thousand bird species, including harpy eagles and musk pheasants, the forest offers a great opportunity to witness the bird diversity of the region.

Flora of the Amazon: Discover the diversity of the rainforest, from hardwoods to medicinal plants used by indigenous communities. The walk gives an insight into the relationship between animals and fauna.

Rurrenabaque: End your Amazon jungle exploration in Rurrenabaque, a town on the banks of the Beni River. Relax, reflect on your jungle adventure, and maybe take another trip, like a wildlife tour to nearby Pampa.

Conservation efforts: Pay attention to cultural practices of tourism and contribute to the preservation of the Amazon rainforest. Protect local ecosystems, follow travel advisories, and support leaders who are important in protecting these precious resources.

Bolivia's Amazon rainforest invites you to discover its mysteries, listen to the music of nature and witness the magic of biodiversity in its purest form. When you go into the green labyrinth of this extraordinary ecosystem, you will see a world arranged with life and beauty that will leave your heart, and you will learn about the diversity of our world. ¡ Bienvenidos of Amazonía Bolivia! (Welcome to the Bolivian Amazon!)

Lake Titicaca

Discover the incredible beauty and culture of Lake Titicaca, the jewel between Bolivia and Peru, known for its deep, spiritual indigenous culture and beautiful landscape.

Jewel of High Altitude: Lake Titicaca rises to an altitude of over 3,800 meters (12,500 feet), making it one of the highest lakes in the world. Its crystal clear waters are surrounded by the highest mountains of the Andes.

Spiritual connection: Lake Titicaca was revered and considered sacred by ancient Andean cultures. According to Inca mythology, this is believed to be the birthplace of the sun god Inti. Its deep cultural history adds to the lake's mystical appeal.

Copacabana: Begin your mission in the town of Copacabana near the beach. Visit the Cathedral of Our Lady of Copacabana, a major pilgrimage site, and witness the fusion of Catholic and indigenous rituals.

Isla del Sol (Island of the Sun): Sail to Isla del Sol, the legendary island believed to be the birthplace of the Inca civilization. Explore ancient Incan ruins, terraced hillsides and enjoy panoramic views of the lake.

Isla de la Luna (Island of the Moon): Continue your island exploration at Isla de la Luna, famous for its archaeological sites and the Temple of Our Lady. According to legend, the island was the shelter of Inca priestesses.

Reed Boat Experience: Meet the Uru people who live on floating islands made of Tortola reeds. Take a traditional boat tour to understand the lifestyle of the Uru people and witness their harmony with Lake Titicaca.

Puno Gateway to Lake Titicaca: Enter Peru to visit Puno, the city that is the gateway to the Peruvian side of Lake Titicaca. Explore local shops and attend the Festival of Our Lady of Candelaria if your travel plan allows.

Tortola Reed Crafts: Discover the art of Tortola Reed Crafts. The local community is skilled in using natural fibers to weave similar items such as boats, mats and decorative items, preserving their ancient skills.

Unique Biodiversity: Lake Titicaca is home to a unique area of flora and fauna adapted to its highest point. Witness birds such as Andean geese and admire Tortola's reed beds, which provide a perfect location.

Homestay Experience: Immerse yourself in local culture with a homestay on the shores of Lake Titicaca. Share food, stories and daily life with Aboriginal families for an authentic and meaningful experience.

A blend of philosophy and culture, Lake Titicaca invites you to discover its shores, islands and culture. Whether you're looking for a spiritual connection, a sense of history, or tranquility, the timeless pool will satisfy your desire. ¡Bienvenidos al Lago Titicaca: you need a Webtalk page! (Welcome to Lake Titicaca!)

Hiking and Trekking

Embark on an adventure in Bolivia, a place full of wondrous experiences, from highaltitude Andean peaks to lush rainforest trails. Lace up your sandals and discover the wonders of nature that await you.

Cordillera Real: For high altitude hiking, head to the Cordillera Real, part of the Andes Mountains. Explore trails that lead to beautiful glacial lakes, rugged peaks and Andean villages.

Huayna Potosi Hike: If you're looking for a challenging but rewarding hike, consider climbing Huayna Potosi, a glacier peak near La Paz. The trail offers breathtaking views of the Sierra Real and more than 6,000 meters (19,685 feet) of climbing.

Taxiway: Follow in the ancient footsteps of the Incas on the Taxiway, the historic Inca route connecting the Andes to the Amazon. The road offers a journey from high altitude to cloud forest, passing through different ecosystems.

Choro Trek: Another classic hiking route from the Andes to the Amazon is the Choro Trek. This multiday adventure will take you through changing landscapes such as towering mountains, hot springs, and dense forests.

Kondorili Base Camp: Travel to Kondorili Base Camp, surrounded by towering peaks and pristine alpine lakes.

The Kondoriri massif offers a beautiful landscape for hikers seeking beauty and adventure.

Sajama National Park: Explore Sajama National Park and hike among snowcapped volcanoes, hot springs and unique plants. The park is home to Bolivia's highest mountain, Nevado Sajama, and offers many hiking trails.

Ambolo National Park: Walk through the Amazon Basin in Ambolo National Park. Walk through the dense forest and discover the diverse wildlife, waterfalls and rich biodiversity of this unique ecosystem.

Torotoro National Park: If you want to visit another part of the world, visit Torotoro National Park. Walk through this beautiful place and explore deep canyons, limestone caves and dinosaur tracks.

Apollobamba Trek: Hike in the Apollobamba Mountains combining high altitude challenges with encounters with indigenous communities. Experience the rich culture of the region as you pass through mountain passes and visit remote villages.

Yunga Cruz Trek: Yunga Cruz Trek connects the high Andes to the Yungas region. Pass through the cloud forest from the mountain and enjoy the transition from mountain scenery to subtropical landscape.

Hiking Tips:

Altitude Acclimatization: Bolivia's high altitude requires acclimatization; Take some time to recover before embarking on a difficult journey.

Essentials Pack: Bring adequate water, snacks, weatherappropriate clothing, first aid kit and orientation tools.

Local Guide: Hire a local guide for safer, more efficient travel, especially in remote areas.

Responsible Hiking: Pay attention to local ecosystems, follow the chosen route; There is no way to preserve Bolivia's untouched nature.

Whether you're climbing the mountains of the Andes, traversing ancient trails, or exploring the Amazon rainforest, Bolivia's hiking and backpacking opportunities guarantee your adventure across cultures. A view that reveals the diversity of the country at every step of change. Thank you! (Have a nice trip!)

Mountain Biking

Get ready for an adrenalinepumping adventure to explore Bolivia's diverse landscapes on two wheels. Mountain bikers will find the park full of fun, challenging trails and beautiful views. Here's your guide to experiencing Bolivia's mountain bike trails:

Camino de la Muerte: Get ready for one of the world's most epic mountain bike trails on Camino de la Muerte. Depart La Paz and descend through the highlands towards the subtropical Yungas along narrow mountain roads.

The World's Most Dangerous Road: The Road to Death earned the reputation of "The World's Most Dangerous Road" due to its narrow roads, cliffs and unpredictable weather conditions. Today it has become a popular route for thrill seekers looking for an unforgettable journey.

Chacaltaya Downhill: Start your journey at the old Chacaltaya ski resort, once the highest ski resort in the world. Descend an exciting route more than

5,000 meters (16,400 feet) above sea level and enjoy the beauty of the Andes.

Sorata to Koroyco: The beginning of an epic multiday cycling adventure from Sorata to Koroyco. This route will take you to different landscapes such as high mountains, dense forests and beautiful villages.

Sajama National Park: Explore the trails of Sajama National Park by mountain bike. Pass through high mountains surrounded by snowcapped peaks, hot springs and geological formations.

Isla del Sol Trail: Explore a bike path combining cultural exploration with highaltitude climbing on Isla del Sol on Lake Titicaca. Drive along the ancient Inca road and enjoy panoramic views of the lake.

La Paz City Downhill: Have fun at La Paz City Downhill. Descend from the highrise neighborhoods to the big city, making your way through the city's steep streets and challenges.

Cordillera Real Traverse: For a true Andean mountain biking adventure, consider the Cordillera Real Traverse. This multiday journey takes you through high mountains, rural villages and mountain landscapes.

Apolloba Circuit: Combine mountain biking with cultural activities at Apolloba Circuit. Walk in the mountains and visit indigenous communities in a region rich in tradition and natural beauty.

Important Tips:

Good Equipment: Keep your mountain bike in good condition and use appropriate safety equipment, including a helmet and protective clothing.

Altitude Statement: Bolivia's altitude needs improvement; Climb slowly to higher altitudes to avoid altitude sickness.

Guide: Leave a report on the difficulty of the road, especially on remote roads, to be safe and travel unknown.

Seasonal Planning: Check the weather forecast and plan your adventure bike ride seasonally to avoid extreme weather conditions.

Whether you're conquering the legendary mountain ranges of the Death Road or exploring the remote trails of the Andes, mountain biking in Bolivia makes for a fun ride. So grab your gear, enjoy the beautiful scenery, and let the thrill of Bolivia's mountain biking guide you. Thank you! (Have a good journey!)

Wildlife Encounters

Embark on a journey through the diverse ecosystems of Bolivia, where wildlife thrives in the heart of the Andes, the Amazon rainforest and especially the high altitude landscapes. Here is your guide to unforgettable wildlife in Bolivia:

Madidi National Park: Discover the biological treasures of Madidi National Park. Madidi is home to many animal species, including jaguars, macaws and capybaras, and its lush forests and Andean foothills provide a rich biodiversity.

Ambrose National Park: Work in Ambrose National Park, where the cloud forest hides many animal species. From lively hummingbirds to elusive ocelots, the park's diverse habitats provide a haven for wildlife lovers.

Amazon River Dolphins: Explore the waters of the Amazon basin and see the beautiful Amazon dolphins. These pink and gray dolphins provide a beautiful and entertaining sight as they dazzlingly cross the river.

Sajama National Park: Explore the highaltitude wildlife of Sajama National Park, where camels and Andean camels roam the high plateau. The park's unique flora and fauna have adapted to the challenges of living at the highest altitude.

Bird watching in Torotoro National Park: Torotoro National Park is not famous for its geological wonders; It is also a paradise for bird watchers. Watch colorful toucans, parrots and the elusive Andean vultures soar above the idyllic park.

Flamingo Lagoon in Uyuni: Travel to the surreal landscape surrounding Salar de Uyuni, where the pink lagoon attracts thousands of flamingos. Watch these beautiful birds pass through shallow waters against the peaks of the Andes Mountains.

Chalalan Ecolodge, Madidi: Stay at Chalalan Ecolodge in Madidi National Park and enjoy a unique blend of ecotourism and wildlife encounters. Wake up to the sounds of the forest and enter the forest with an experienced guide to see monkeys, tapirs and countless bird species.

Andean Condor Viewing: Head to the Andean peaks, especially the Colca Canyon, for the chance to watch the majestic Andean Condor in flight. The birds' huge wings and aerial acrobatics create a sense of excitement.

Reserva Eduardo Avaroa: In the highaltitude landscapes of Reserva Eduardo Avaroa, encounter unique wildlife adapted to extreme conditions. Keep an eye out for vicuñas, Andean geese, and the elusive viscacha, a rabbitlike rodent.

The Pampas: Navigate the pampas (plains) in the Amazon Basin for encounters with capybaras, caimans, and a variety of bird species. Night tours add extra excitement by offering the opportunity to see nocturnal animals.

Responsible Wildlife: Participate in responsible wildlife tourism by choosing ecofriendly accommodations and tour guides that lead to the protection and respect of habitats. Follow wildlife care ethics and maintain a safe distance to avoid harming animals. Bolivia's diverse ecosystems promise encounters with extraordinary wildlife.

From the depths of the Amazon to the heights of the Andes, each region shows a different natural character. So keep your mind sharp, pay attention to what's available, and get ready to enjoy Bolivia's incredible wildlife. ¡ Long live biodiversity! (Long live biodiversity!)

Chapter 6. Indigenous Cultures and MustSee Destinations

Traditional Festivals

Bolivia's rich cultural fabric comes alive with beautiful and diverse performances where local customary laws, music, dance and religious rituals combine to create a beautiful display of cultural heritage. Some of Bolivia's most interesting festivals include:

Oruro Carnival:

Where: Oruro

When: February or March

Highlights: Oruro Carnival is on the World Heritage List as a UNESCO World Heritage Site , this masterpiece is dazzling. The show combines Andean national traditions with Catholic rituals. Witness colorful parades, elaborate costumes and traditional dances for St. Sokhavin.

Gran Poder Festival:

Where: La Paz

When: May or June

Highlights: The Gran Poder Festival is a presentation of La Paz culture. Participants wore bright costumes and paraded through the streets, performing traditional costumes, celebrating Andean stories, and showing their passion for music.

Feast of the Virgin Mary:

Where: Copacabana, Puno (Peru)

When: February

Highlights: Celebrated in Bolivia and Peru, this festival honors Our Lady of Candelaria. Pilgrims take part in parades, traditional dances and ceremonies that create a colorful and lively atmosphere.

Fiesta de la Cruz:

Where: All of Bolivia

When: May 3,

Highlights: Fiesta de la Cruz, or Feast of the Cross print. The elaborate ceremony consists of processions, music, and the making of beautiful crosses. It combines preColumbian traditions with Catholicism.

Corpus Christi:

Where: Pujllay, Tarabuco, Tarija and other places

When: May or June

Highlights: Sti. Perth Christie celebrations vary by region. For example, in Tarabuco there is a local dance and celebration, while in Tarija there is a celebration and traditional music in the celebration.

Feast of San Juan:

Where: Titicaca District

When: June 24,

Highlights: on the summer solstice, San Juan Feast, Where is the Sun, pays homage to Inti. Celebrations include feasts, dancing and bonfires as communities come together to welcome the new agricultural cycle.

Diablada Festival:

Location: All over Bolivia

Time: A few days

Highlights: The Diablada, or Devil's Dance, is a popular dance performed at many festivals. Folkloric dance, especially in Oruro. The dancers wear beautiful devil costumes, showing a mix of Aboriginal and Christian beliefs.

Fiesta del Gran Poder Indígena Originario:

Location: Sucre

Time: Last week of May

Highlights: Locals Sucre Celebration in homage to Pachamama (Mother)'s gift to the world). Participants form a deep connection with the natural world by participating in ceremonies, dances and performances.

Fiesta del Señor Jesús del Gran Poder:

Where: La Paz

When: May or June

Main content: Another Gran Poder festivities event Officially, this event in La Paz hosts a huge parade with thousands of participants, presenting the city's culture with dance and music.

Tojorokas Festival:

Where: Tarabuco

When: August 1,

Highlights: Tojorokas is the local celebration of Tarabuco Pachamama is a festival. The event, where participants wear colorful costumes reflecting the culture of the region, includes music, dance and celebration.

Bolivia's traditional festivals are a true testament to the richness of the country's culture and the harmony between its indigenous people and colonial influences. These celebrations provide a unique window into Bolivia's diverse communities, their spirituality, and their longstanding ties to their past. Long live tradition! (Long live tradition!)

Local Markets

Bolivia's local markets are lively places where the country's different cultures come together to enjoy the colours, smells and sounds of daily life. Immerse yourself in the vibrant atmosphere as you explore some of Bolivia's most fascinating markets:

Witches Market (Mercado de las Brujas):

Location: La Paz

Highlights: The Devil's Market in La Paz is known for its mysterious location and is a treasure trove of Andean medicine. , herbs and amulets. Look for unique stalls, festive items and alpaca fetuses believed to bring good luck.

Mercado Rodríguez:

Location: La Paz

Highlights: Stop by Mercado Rodríguez for an extraordinary thrill. From fresh produce and snacks to handicrafts and textiles, this market is a small sampling of daily life in La Paz.

Mercado Central:

Location: Sucre

Highlights: Mercado Central in Sucre is a food court offering a variety of fresh fruits, vegetables and meat and local delicacies. The market also displays beautiful textiles and traditional clothing.

Tarabuco Market:

Location: Tarabuco

Highlights: Tarabuco is famous for its Sunday market, where indigenous communities display their crafts, crafts and artistic products. traditional clothes, whole life. This is an exhibition of Bolivian craftsmanship and heritage.

Mercado de San Francisco:

Location: La Paz

Highlights: Mercado de San Francisco is a large market in the heart of La Paz. lots of fresh produce, spices and local cuisine. Explore the maze of shops and experience real local life.

Mercado de los Pozos:

Location: Cochabamba

Highlights: Mercado de los Pozos in Cochabamba is famous for its variety of fruits, trees and vegetables. spice. Chat with vendors, taste local snacks, and witness the colorful beauty of Andean traditions.

Potosí Market:

Location: Potosí

Highlights : Potosí Market is a meeting point of culture and embodies the important history of the city. Explore shops selling silver, textiles and handicrafts, and learn about Potosi's history.

Mercado Campesino:

Location: Sucre

Highlights: Sucre's Mercado Campesino is a large marketplace where farmers from the surrounding area gather to sell their produce. is the market. . From fresh fruits and vegetables to handcrafted goods, the market showcases the region's rich agricultural resources.

Mercado Excentral:

Location: Santa Cruz

Highlights: Mercado Excentral in Santa Cruz is the market you come to. New products for handicrafts. Taste local delicacies and witness the diverse culture of the region.

de Julio Market:

Location: El Alto

Highlights: One of the largest markets in South America, El Alto's 16 de Julio Market is a large area of shops selling a wide range of products, from Traditional Andean textiles to electronics. Know the power of this moving business.

When you visit a local market in Bolivia, you will encounter many products and have the opportunity to connect with the different cultures that make up the country's identity. From traditional textiles to exotic spices, each market is a unique expression of Bolivia's rich heritage. Welcome to the Market! (Welcome to the store!)

Interacting with Indigenous Communities

Engaging with Bolivia's indigenous communities offers a profound opportunity to immerse yourself in the country's rich cultural tapestry. Respectful interactions can lead to meaningful exchanges and a deeper understanding of the traditions, customs, and daily lives of these diverse communities. Here are some tips for a culturally sensitive and enriching experience:

Respect Local Customs:

Greeting Etiquette: Learn and use basic greetings in the local language, such as Quechua or Aymara, to show respect.

Handshakes, nods, or traditional greetings vary among different communities.

Attend Community Events:

Festivals and Ceremonies: If you are able to attend a local festival or ceremony, please ask if you can watch or participate. Many Aboriginal communities are proud to share their traditions.

Ask permission to take photos:

Ask first: Don't forget to ask for permission before taking photos. Some communities may have beliefs about photography and it is important to respect their views.

Support Local Artisans:

Buy Crafts: Support your health by purchasing crafts directly from local experts. This includes textiles, pottery and traditional products made by local people.

Homestay Experience:

Local Life: Consider a homestay to experience daily life in the community. This not only provides an authentic experience, but also directly supports the local economy.

Learning Traditional Foods:

Sharing the meal: If invited, accept the invitation to join the meal. This promotes a sense of hospitality and allows you to sample local delicacies while engaging in meaningful conversations.

Ask questions respectfully:

Ask respectfully for curiosity: It always arouses curiosity, but please ask questions carefully, thinking well about leadership. Enjoy learning about their traditions, beliefs and lifestyle.

Learning Important Words:

Communication: Although many indigenous people in Bolivia speak Spanish, learning two or three words in your own language goes a long way in resolving this situation can. communication.

Travel Support:

Mission Travel: Select a mission and community worker. These measures are important for sustainable practices and directly contribute to the health of local communities.

Personal Education:

Cultural Awareness: Before your visit, please educate yourself about the culture and history of the community you plan to visit. Understanding their background can improve your ability to interact respectfully.

Obey the customs of the society:

Pay attention to manners: Pay attention to all customs and manners of the society, such as removing shoes before entering the house or attending a public event.

Say Thank You:

Say Thank You: Thank you for your hospitality and knowledge. A simple thankyou can go a long way in building positive connections. Remember, the key to meaningful interactions with indigenous communities is a genuine interest in learning, respecting their way of life, and fostering connections based on mutual understanding.

By approaching these experiences with an open heart and cultural sensitivity, you can create lasting memories and contribute positively to the communities you encounter. ¡Buena convivencia! (Good coexistence!)

Sucre

Located at the foot of the Andes Mountains and also known as "La Ciudad Blanca" (The White City), Sucre is the official capital of Bolivia and a UNESCO World Heritage Site. This fascinating city is home to rich historical heritage, colonial architecture and beautiful culture. Here are the reasons why Sucre is a must visit:

Colonial Elegance: Sucre's historic center is a showcase of preserved colonial beauty. Walk along narrow cobblestone streets lined with white houses adorned with wroughtiron balconies, creating a constant atmosphere.

Casa de la Libertad: Visit Casa de la Libertad, where Bolivia signed its declaration of independence in 1825. The museum contains important artifacts and documents regarding the country's early history.

Plaza 25 de Mayo: Central square Plaza 25 de Mayo is the heart of Sucre. Surrounded by important buildings such as the Metropolitan Cathedral and the Government Palace, the square is the meeting point of locals and tourists.

Sucre Cathedral: Discover Sucre Cathedral, a beautiful building with a beautiful interior. Marvel at its opulent decoration, religious art and panoramic views of the city from the bell tower.

San Felipe Neri Monastery: Explore the colonial church San Felipe Neri Monastery, now the ASSYR Textile Museum. The museum presents beautiful materials and modern techniques from different regions of Bolivia.

Tarabuco Market: Head to the nearby Tarabuco Market on Sundays to experience indigenous culture. Famous for its textiles and handicrafts, this market is a colorful place where locals can trade goods and celebrate their heritage.

Dinosaur Footprints: Just outside Sucre, the Cal Orck'o escarpment has one of the largest collections of dinosaur prints in the world. Walk along the cliffs and witness more than 5,000 footprints dating back millions of years.

Universities in Sucre: Sucre is home to many universities, creating a young and dynamic environment. Take a walk in Bolivar Park, a popular park for students and active activities.

Mercado Campesino: Explore Mercado Campesino and experience local life and flavors. This supermarket stocks fresh produce, snacks and gives you a real view of daily activities.

Cafe Culture: There is a thriving cafe culture in Sucre. Relax with a cup of Bolivian coffee in one of the many charming cafes and enjoy the relaxing atmosphere surrounded by colonial architecture.

Local Festivals: If you can meet a local celebration like the Carnival of Our Lady of Guadalupe, you will see performances of beautiful things, traditional dances and beautiful places. Sucre's combination of history, culture and natural beauty make it a great destination for travelers seeking a unique Bolivian experience.

Whether you walk its colonial streets or explore its treasures, Sucre invites you to a world where past and present intertwine. ¡Bienvenido and Sucre! (Welcome to Sucre!)

Potosi

Situated high in the Andes, Potosi is a testament to the impact of Bolivia's colonial past and its immense mineral wealth. Known as the "Silver City", Potosi is one of the largest and richest cities in the world. Here's a look at the charm of Potosi:

Cerro Rico: At the heart of Potosi lies the "rich mountain" Cerro Rico. This mountain was a rich source of money during the colonial period and led to the success of the Spanish Empire. Today it is a symbol of wealth and economy.

Casa Nacional de la Moneda: Take a look at Casa Nacional de la Moneda, built in 1759 to handle large amounts of money mined from Cerro Rico. The colonialera building now serves as a museum, housing artifacts and demonstrating the coinage process.

Historic Sites: Walk through the UNESCO World Heritage Historical Center of Potosi, where colonial buildings and narrow streets take you back in time. The Cathedral of Our Lady of Peace dominates the middle of November 10 Square with its magnificent façade.

Potosi Silver Mine: Visit the Cerro Rico silver mine and learn more about Potosi's mining heritage. Tours offer the opportunity to go deep into the tunnels, witness the hard work and learn about the miners' lifestyle.

Santa Teresa Convent Museum: Visit the Santa Teresa Convent Museum, an 18thcentury convent that presents the life of Carmelite nuns. The museum houses religious art and artifacts and has panoramic views of the city.

La Cruz Mountain Lookout: Hike to La Cruz Mountain Lookout and enjoy beautiful panoramic views of Potosi and the surrounding landscape. The city's red roof tiles create a beautiful backdrop against the backdrop of Mount Rico.

San Francisco Church: Explore the San Francisco Church, an iconic religious site with a baroque facade. The church has a beautiful altar decorated with gold leaf, reflecting the wealth of the region.

Mercado Central: Immerse yourself in local life at Mercado Central in Potosi. The market showcases design, textiles and traditional handicrafts from the region. A great place to experience the daily challenges of the city.

Mint House Rooftop: Climb to the roof of the Mint House for a panoramic view of Potosi. This landscape offers a unique view of the urban environment surrounded by Andean peaks.

Tradition: If your visit coincides with local festivals such as the Potosi Carnival, you will see a colorful festival of parades, traditional dances and live shows showcasing the city's heritage.

Mineralogical Museum: Explore the Mineralogical Museum and marvel at the dazzling collection of minerals and gemstones showcasing the geological diversity of the Potosi region. Potosi's heritage as a silver mining center and colonial architecture create a place steeped in history.

The city's beautiful scenery and rich culture make it a great destination for travelers looking for a combination of heritage and discovery. ¡ In Potosí! (Welcome to Potosi!)

Rurrenabaque

Located in northern Bolivia, Rurrenabaque is the main gateway to the untouched regions of the Amazon Basin. Located at the confluence of the Beni and Rurrenabaque Rivers, this vibrant city offers a unique blend of Amazonian adventure, indigenous culture and stunning biodiversity.

Amazon Jungle Tour: Rurrenabaque is the beginning of an unforgettable adventure in the Amazon jungle. Embark on a walking tour to explore lush rainforests, winding rivers, and diverse ecosystems. Wildlife enthusiasts can meet many species, from playful monkeys to powerful birds.

Madidi National Park: Madidi National Park, accessible by boat from Rurrenabaque, is one of the most biodiverse areas in the world. Explore lush forests that are home to jaguars, tapirs, macaws and countless other species.

Educational tours give you the opportunity to immerse yourself in such a feeling.

Pampas Tour: Explore nearby Pampas, a vast area filled with flowing lakes and rivers. Pampas tours offer the opportunity to see caimans, capybaras, red dolphins and many bird species. This is a unique and peaceful situation in the Amazon.

Aboriginal Culture: Rurrenabaque is surrounded by Aboriginal communities, including the Takana and Chimane people. Visitors can participate in cultural exchange and learn about culture, religion and the community's deep connection to the forest.

Beni River: Beni River flows through Rurrenabaque and offers good sailing. Sail the waters to witness coastal communities, see coastal wildlife, and experience life in the Amazon Basin.

Rurrenabaque Wildlife Sanctuary: In Rurrenabaque, visit the Rurrenabaque Wildlife Sanctuary to see animals rescued in the area. The conservation center serves as a rehabilitation center and learning center to promote conservation.

Yakuma River: Explore the Yakuma River, a tributary of the Amazon, on a boat tour. This pristine river weaves through lush green scenery, providing opportunities for bird watching and encountering a variety of aquatic species.

Local Cuisine: Enjoy Amazonian cuisine in Rurrenabaque. Try dishes featuring fresh fish from the river, exotic fruits and unique flavors of the Amazon region.

Flora of the Bolivian Amazon: The Bolivian Amazon is a wonder and Rurrenabaque is the best starting point for nature lovers. Witness the different types of plants, grasses and trees that make the forest diverse in terms of biodiversity.

Sustainable Tourism Initiatives: Rurenabac has seen an increase in sustainable tourism initiatives that promote responsible travel and conservation. Choosing ecofriendly tours and services that are important for the health of the Amazon ecosystem is not easy.

Jungle Lodge: Experience the Amazon from the comfort of one of the jungles around Rurrenabaque. These hotels combine fun with relaxation, allowing you to immerse yourself in nature without the freedom of animals. Rurrenabaque attracts those who want to experience the real Amazon, where the music of the jungle, encounters with diverse wildlife and connections to indigenous cultures create memories that last forever.

Whether exploring the jungle, boating along the river, or interacting with local communities, Rureña Baque opens the door to the imagination of the Bolivian

Amazon. Welcome to the Bolivian Amazon! (Welcome to the Bolivian Amazon!)

Chapter 7. Hidden Gems and Bolivian Cuisine

OfftheBeatenPath Towns

With its diverse landscapes and wealth, Bolivia hides a variety of offthebeatenpath cities that offer exclusive knowledge and special knowledge. Take a look at a littleknown corner of the country. Here are some hidden gems waiting to be discovered:

Samaipata: Located in the eastern foothills of the Andes, Samaipata is famous for its archaeological site El Fuerte. The preInca ceremonial site features intricate carvings and spectacular views of the surrounding valley.

Toro Toro: Toro Toro is a small town at the foot of the Andes, where Bolivia's first expedition was located. Explore the giant dinosaur tracks of

ToroToro National Park, including caves and beautiful forests.

Villa de Leyva: Villa de Leyva is the colonial jewel of the Chiquitanía district with its wellpreserved buildings, cobblestone streets and huge Plaza Ruler. Surrounded by natural beauties, the city is a peaceful place.

Curahuara de Carangas: Curahuara de Carangas is a colonial town that is home to the beautiful San Pedro de Curahuara church, House of San Pedro de Cuba. This historic church, decorated with beautiful frescoes, is one of the oldest churches in Bolivia and shows Andean and Spanish influences.

Tomarapi: Located in the highlands of Bolivia, Tomarapi is a small agricultural village famous for its special agricultural terraces or "andenes". These terraces reflect ancient agricultural techniques that continue to sustain the community.

Tupisa: Known for its red landscape reminiscent of the American Southwest, Tupisa offers a combination of cowboy culture and magnificent scenery. Explore the canyons, gorges and historical sites around the city.

Chalazani: Chalazani is located in northern Bolivia and is the gateway to the Apollobamba Mountains. This rural town offers opportunities to enjoy beautiful scenery, traditional festivals and interact with Aboriginal communities.

San Ignacio de Velasco: San Ignacio de Velasco is located in the heart of Chiquitanía, Bolivia, known for its Jesuit missions and traditions. Explore the historic destination, enjoy local music and discover a unique blend of Aboriginal and colonial influences.

Reyes: Located in the Amazon Basin, Reyes is the gateway to Madidi National Park. This peaceful town allows you to experience the rich biodiversity of the

Amazon while providing a base for jungle adventures.

Ravello: Located in the valley near Cochabamba, Ravello is a peaceful place surrounded by rice terraces, historic churches and eucalyptus groves. This is the best place for those looking for peace.

Apollo: Located in northern Bolivia, Apollo is a rural town surrounded by dense forests and rivers. It is the starting point for exploring Madidi National Park, where there are many species of animals and fauna waiting to be discovered.

Puerto Villarroel: Located on the banks of the Ichilo River, Puerto Villarroel is a peaceful town surrounded by greenery. Provides peace of mind for recreation and water sports. Explore Bolivia's offthebeatenpath cities and learn about the country's diverse geography, rich history and passion of local communities.

These hidden gems give you the chance to escape the crowds and embrace the true, lesserknown side of Bolivia. Explain the mystery of Bolivia! (Discover Bolivia's hidden treasures!)

Secret Natural Spots

With its diverse ecosystems and diverse landscapes, Bolivia is home to hidden natural attractions off the beaten path, just waiting to be discovered by intrepid travelers. Here are some of the paradises where nature is at its most beautiful:

Laguna Verde: Located in the southwestern part of Bolivia, Laguna Verde is a beautiful, high lake surrounded by snowcapped peaks. Vibrant green water set against the backdrop of the Andes Mountains creates a surreal and breathtaking view.

Maragua Crater: Hidden in a valley near Sucre, Maragua Crater is a marvel. Walk through the beautiful landscape and discover this hidden gem, where ancient stones and traditional Quechua villages await you.

Laguna Glacial Chiar Khota: Located deep in the Royal Mountains, Laguna Glacial Chiar Khota is a pristine glacial lake surrounded by towering peaks. Offering unique mountain beauty to adventurers, this hidden treasure can be reached with a challenging hike.

Cueva del Diablo: Travel to a remote area of Toro Toro National Park to find Cueva del Diablo, a cave full of stalactite and stalagmite formations. Exploring this underground world is a unique and mysterious experience.

Aguas Termales de Polques: Located near Salar de Uyuni, Aguas Termales de Polques are natural hot springs surrounded by a surreal landscape. Relax in the healing waters while admiring the vast Salar de Uyuni.

Maragua Crater: Maragua Crater is a hidden volcanic crater near Tarija, surrounded by lush vegetation and colorful landscapes. The Caldera's tranquility and offbeat charm make it a paradise for nature lovers.

Lago Colorada (Red Lagoon): Salar de Uyuni attracts many people's attention, but nearby Lago Colorada is still a surprise. The red color of the lake, caused by algae and mineral deposits, contrasts with the large white salt surrounding it.

Laguna Azul (Blue Lagoon): Located deep in Madidi National Park, Laguna Azul is a hidden gem accessible through untouched forest. The calm waters of the lake reflect the emerald beauty of the Amazon River, providing a secluded oasis.

Aguas Calientes: Aguas Calientes, located in the Bolivian Amazon, is a nature secret famous for its hot springs. Surrounded by lush forests, these hot springs offer a refreshing experience amidst the sounds of the forest.

Serranía de Hornocal: Near the city of Humahuaca, across the border from Argentina, the Serranía de Hornocal reveals a hidden treasure: a beautiful mountain with fourteen colors. This geological phenomenon is the wellkept secret of the heights.

Lake Poopó: Often overshadowed by its larger neighbor, Lake Titicaca, Lake Poopó is a peaceful and secluded place. The flat coast and bird diversity offer a peaceful escape from the usual sightseeing.

Laguna Huayñacota: Located deep in the Yongas region, Laguna Huayñacota is a hidden gem surrounded by cloud forests.

This clean lake is a peaceful place, away from the chaos and with a beautiful view.

Discover Bolivia's hidden places that reveal the unique beauty of the country and give you the opportunity to come into contact with incredible landscapes. As you adventure across the map, you'll experience the magic of Bolivia's hidden paradise, each offering a unique aspect of the country's imagination. Discover Deconocido! (Do you want to know the mystery!)

Unique Experiences

With its diverse landscapes and culture, Bolivia offers many unique experiences beyond the original. For those looking for a unique adventure, here are some extraordinary activities that are expected to leave a lasting impression:

Sailing on the highest navigable lake: Located at over 12,000 feet above sea level, Lake Titicaca offers a unique sailing experience. Sail into clear waters, visit the Uros Islands and witness the beauty of the world's highest navigable lake.

Ride the Safest Road in the World: Known as the "Road of Death", the Yungas road near La Paz offers a thrilling ride. Descend from the highaltitude plateau to the warm and lush Yungas for an exciting and adrenalinepumping descent.

Stargazing at Salar de Uyuni: Experience the magic of the night sky at the vast Salar de Uyuni. Bolivia's mountainous regions have minimal light pollution and stars everywhere, creating a stargazing wonder, especially at night.

Traditional Boat Tour of the Amazon Pampas: Take a boat out onto the waters of the Amazon Pampas. This experience allows you to explore the rich biodiversity of the Bolivian Amazon while enjoying the tranquility of the jungle.

Visit the world's largest salt flat: Salar de Uyuni is the world's largest salt flat, offering a horizondisappearing experience. During the rainy season, a thin layer of water turns the flat salt into a large mirror, creating a beautiful reflection.

Join the Oruro Carnival: Immerse yourself in the vibrant Oruro Carnival, a UNESCO World Heritage Site. Featuring lavish costumes, traditional dances and fascinating displays of rich culture, this dazzling celebration combines Aboriginal traditions with Catholic rituals.

Toro Toro Dinosaur Tracks Quest: Start a journey to Toro Toro National Park to find dinosaur tracks preserved in rocks. This archaeological adventure takes you back in time and gives you a glimpse into the prehistoric world.

Take the death train by train (Ferroviaria Oriental): Take the Ferroviaria Oriental, known as the "Death Train", in the rugged region of Chiquitania, Bolivia. This tour offers unique views of the historical district, with beautiful views along the way.

Lake Titicaca Floating Island Homestay: Spend the night on the floating islands of Lake Titicaca and experience the true hospitality of Uru. This immersive homestay introduces you to Aboriginal culture and lifestyle.

Southwest Circuit Jeep tour: Explore the rugged beauty of the Bolivia Southwest Circuit with a Jeep tour. Witness beautiful scenery, colorful lakes and unique rocks, including the surreal Salvador Dali desert.

Explore Incahuasi Island in the Salar de Uyuni: Incahuasi Island, also known as "Fish Island", stands like a reef in the middle of the Salar de Uyuni.

Explore this unique ecosystem full of towering cacti and enjoy panoramic views of the salt flats.

Jolita Wrestling in La Paz: Attend Jolita Wrestling in La Paz, where local women perform their wrestling in traditional costumes. This fun and inspiring experience will give you a unique insight into Bolivia's important culture.

The unique experience in Bolivia is not only an unforgettable adventure, but also a connection to the country's diversity and beautiful culture. Whether sailing on a highaltitude lake, cycling along the Death Road, or stargazing on the salt flats, each activity reflects a different facet of Bolivia's interests. i Long live the experience! (Save special experience!)

Culinary Traditions

Bolivia's culinary landscape is a vibrant tapestry of flavours, local ingredients and traditions. From the highaltitude Andes to the Amazon lowlands, Bolivia's culinary traditions reflect the country's rich history and diversity.

Quinoa: Quinoa is an important ingredient in Andean cuisine and has a sacred place in Bolivian tradition. Quinoa is available in many forms, from soups to salads, and is not only a food crop, but is also deeply rooted in local agriculture.

Salteñas: These cakes are similar to empanadas and contain a delicious mixture of meat, potatoes, peas and spices. Salteñas generally have the right balance of slightly sweet and salty, making them a favorite for breakfast and lunch.

Anticuchos: Originating from preColumbian times, Anticuchos are kebabs usually made from beef heart, marinated and grilled. Skewers served with potatoes or corn are a good example of ethnic cooking.

Silpancho: Silpancho is a delicious dish originating from Cochabamba, consisting of thin, breaded, fried veal cutlets served with rice and topped with an egg. It offers both national and European cuisine.

Api con Pastel: Api con Pastel is a hot, thick liquid made from purple corn and is a traditional Bolivian breakfast. Often pastel is combined with toasted donuts, creating a cozy and delicious combination.

Pique a lo Macho: Pique a lo macho is a strong and spicy dish that usually includes beef, sausage, onions, tomatoes and peppers. This hearty meat plate represents Bolivia's meatbased tradition.

Chuño: Derived from dried potatoes, chuño has been an important part of the Andean diet for centuries. Chuño is used in many dishes, including soups and stews, that illustrate traditional farming methods adapted to high altitude.

Majadito: Majadito, which comes from the Beni region, is a delicious dish made with rice, beef, onions, tomatoes and spices. Rice is usually cooked until slightly crispy, adding texture to this delicious dish.

Humintas: One of Bolivia's favorite delicacies, humintas are corn huskstuffed balls filled with corn, cheese and spices. This steamed dish incorporates local cooking techniques and local ingredients.

Api Morado: Another variant of api, api morado is a hotblooded corn drink often consumed at festivals. Its rich color and sweet taste make it a popular choice, especially during holidays in Bolivia.

Llajwa: More of a dessert, llajwa is a spicy salsa made from tomatoes, peppers and herbs. It adds a bold, spicy flavor to many dishes, and its popularity has spread throughout Bolivia.

Tarija Wines: Tarija region is famous for its wine production. Enjoy the unique taste of Bolivian wines, especially those made from the country's own grape, Muscat of Alexandria. Bolivian cuisine combines indigenous, Mexican and other cultures to create a diverse and healthy cuisine.

Whether you want to taste the food in the market or savor local delicacies, Bolivia invites you to a culinary journey that reflects the rich culture of the country. Entertainment! (Enjoy your meal!)

Signature Dishes

Bolivia's culinary identity is characterized by a diverse array of flavors and ingredients, resulting in signature dishes that captivate the senses and reflect the country's rich cultural heritage. These iconic dishes have become culinary ambassadors, representing Bolivia's unique gastronomic tapestry:

Salteñas: These savory pastries, filled with a succulent mixture of meat, potatoes, peas, and spices, are a Bolivian breakfast favorite. Salteñas are known for their delicate, slightly sweet dough and are often enjoyed on the go or as a hearty morning treat.

Silpancho: Hailing from Cochabamba, silpancho is a delicious dish consisting of thin, breaded fried steak served with rice. Served with fried eggs and potatoes, this healthy dish represents a fusion of national and European cuisine.

Sajta de Pollo: Sajta de pollo is a spicy and flavorful chicken stew, a traditional Andean dish. Made with chicken, peppers, potatoes and other vegetables, this dish showcases Bolivia's love of rich spices.

Pique a lo Macho: This carnivorous treat is a hearty plate of beef, sausage, onions, tomatoes and peppers. Pique a lo macho is a delicious and spicy dish that reflects the Bolivian passion for courage and abundance.

Charque de Llama: Dried and seasoned camel meat called Charque de llama is a specialty throughout Bolivia. Often used in soups, stews, or simply grilled, charque de llama reflects the country's history of highaltitude pastoralism.

Chairo: A hearty soup originating from the highlands, chairo combines meat (usually beef or lamb) with chuño (freezedried potatoes), vegetables, and spices. This comforting dish has deep roots in indigenous Andean cuisine.

Anticuchos: Marinated and grilled on skewers, anticuchos are a favorite dish. Traditionally made from beef heart, these skewers are seasoned to perfection and often served with potatoes or corn.

Majadito: Majadito is a traditional dish from the Beni region, consisting of a mixture of rice, beef, onions, tomatoes and spices. The rice is cooked until slightly crispy, adding a delicious and comforting texture.

Saice: This spicy and aromatic dish, saice, is a beef stew cooked with tomatoes, chili peppers, and a blend of herbs and spices. It showcases the diverse flavors of Bolivian cuisine, with regional variations adding unique twists.

Cuñape: A popular Bolivian cheese bread, cuñapé is made from yuca (cassava) flour and cheese. Often served as a snack or appetizer, this delicious golden brown dessert reflects Bolivia's use of local ingredients.

Picana: A festive dish often consumed during the holidays, picana is a soup filled with various meats, vegetables, and spices. Its preparation varies from region to region and is a symbol of unity and the celebration of Bolivian unity.

Bolivian Empanadas: There are many regional varieties of Bolivian empanadas, each with its own unique packaging and preparation. Sweet or sour, these handmade snacks showcase the variety of cooking methods unique to Bolivian cuisine.

This special dish is much more than a meal; They are a reflection of Bolivian culture, historical influences and creative use of local materials. Exploring these food items allows you to taste the essence of Bolivia's unique cuisine. Buen Procho! (Enjoy your meal!)

Local Markets and Street Food

Bolivia's local markets and delicious dishes offer a feast for the heart with the smell of spices, the color of fresh produce and the taste of fresh produce Sizzling Grill is a culinary experience creates. Explore these supermarkets and taste a variety of foods that reflect the heart and soul of Bolivia:

Mercado Rodríguez (La Paz): Located in the heart of La Paz, Mercado Rodríguez is a maze of shops selling a variety of Andean products, herbs and spices. Take a break and enjoy local snacks such as salteñas, anticuchos and fresh juices.

Mercado de las Brujas (Witches Market La Paz): Famous for its mystical products and traditional healings, the Witches Market is also a place to eat. Snacks like tucumanas (fried bread) and api (green corn drink) as you explore special areas of the market.

Mercado Central (Sucre): Sucre Central Market is a lively place where locals and tourists can buy fresh produce, meat and spices. Don't miss the opportunity to taste local delicacies such as sausages and empanadas.

Mercado Campesino (Santa Cruz): Located in Santa Cruz, Mercado Campesino showcases the richness of the Bolivian plains. Enjoy street food like salteñas, choripán (grilled hot dogs) and regional dried fruits.

Mercado 16 de Julio (El Alto): Located above La Paz, Mercado 16 de Julio in El Alto is a large market with vendors selling a variety of food products. Sample delicacies like anticuchos, api, and a variety of Andean snacks.

Street Food in Cochabamba: Cochabamba's streets come alive with an array of street food vendors. Try the city's famous dish, silpancho, or snack on savory salteñas and an assortment of grilled meats.

Calle de las Brujas (Potosi): Potosi's Calle de las Brujas turns into a foodie paradise at night. Taste local delicacies such as humintas, tamales and buñuelos to enjoy the unique taste of this towering city.

Tarija Street Food: Famous for its vineyards, Tarija has a culinary experience that complements its wine culture. Sample streetside empanadas, pickles, and local cheeses in this charming southern town.

Trinidad Street Food: Located in the heart of the Bolivian Amazon, Trinidad's food incorporates the tropical flavors of the region. Explore markets selling grilled meats, fresh fish and exotic fruits.

Plaza 25 de Mayo (Sucre): Sucre's central square, Plaza 25 de Mayo, turns into a food lovers' paradise at night. Join locals enjoying picarones (donutlike pastries) and other street food against the backdrop of Sucre's colonial architecture.

Plaza San Francisco (La Paz): Plaza San Francisco in La Paz is the meeting place for food lovers. During the energy of the city, taste snacks such as Anticuchos, salteñas and many other local dishes.

Oruro Street Food: Oruro is famous for its carnival fun, serving healthy street food along with local specialties. Enjoy fried dishes, grilled meats and healthy meals in this city.

Exploring Bolivia's local markets and sampling street food is a fun way to immerse yourself in the country's rich culture. From the traditional flavors of La Paz to the summer flavors of Trinidad, every bite tells the story of Bolivia's culinary heritage. Buen procho en las calles de Bolivia: you need a Webtalk page! (Hello Bolivia's street food!)

8. Practical Tips for Travelers

8.1 Health and Safety

Making sure you're healthy is essential when you travel to Bolivia. Some important health and safety tips for a safe and enjoyable visit:

Elevation Notes: Bolivia's high altitude can pose challenges for visitors. To be successful, on your first date, stay calm, chill, and don't drink too much alcohol. If you have respiratory or heart disease, consult a doctor before traveling.

Water and Food safety: Prepare bottled or clean water to prevent water contamination. When it comes to food, choose hot, fresh foods. Do not eat food on the street that will have to sit for a while, especially in areas where hygiene is a problem.

Vaccinations: Ensure routine vaccinations are completed. Consult a healthcare professional for recommendations on additional vaccinations for your trip, including vaccines for hepatitis A and B, typhoid, and yellow fever.

Sun Protection: Bolivia's high altitude means more sunlight. Use high SPF sunscreen, wear a hat and sunglasses to protect your eyes. Be careful of sunburn, even on foggy days.

Altitude Sickness Medicine: Consider bringing altitude sickness medicine with you if necessary. Talk to your doctor before traveling and be aware of possible side effects. Coca tea has traditionally been used medicinally and is sold in many places.

Safe Transportation: Choose a reputable transportation company, especially for long trips. Follow bus safety rules and avoid traveling at night if possible. If you are going to rent a car, be careful about mountain roads.

Personal Safety: Be alert and aware of your surroundings in crowded areas, especially shopping and tourist areas. Keep your valuables safe, use a money belt and don't leave expensive items behind.

Travel insurance: Get quality travel insurance that covers medical emergencies, trip cancellation, and theft of lost or damaged items. Check if your insurance covers extreme activities and adventure sports.

Weather Planning: Weather in Bolivia varies by region and altitude. Especially if you plan to explore different areas, prepare your suitcase accordingly and be prepared for sudden changes.

Local Medical Centers: Learn the locations of local hospitals and clinics, especially if you are going to a remote area. Carry a first aid kit with essential items like antibiotics, antiinflammatory medications and painkillers.

Prevention of Insects: In areas where there is a risk of mosquito infestation, use insect repellent and wear long shirts and long trousers, especially at dawn and dusk. Consider taking antiinflammatory medication if you are going to visit certain places.

Respect local customs: Respect local customs and traditions. Be respectful of the culture, especially Aboriginal communities, and ask for permission before taking photos. This not only improves your leadership skills but also helps you establish effective interactions.

You can enjoy the beauty and diversity of Bolivia by paying attention to health and safety. Remember, planning and knowledge are the key elements to a successful and profitable trip to this beautiful South American destination. have a good journey! (Safe way!)

Transportation Tips

Traveling to Bolivia's diverse landscapes and vibrant cities requires transportation considerations. Some practical tips to ensure you have a safe and enjoyable journey:

Choose a reputable shipping company: Choose a reputable shipping company, especially for long trips. Choosing a reputable bus company and a reliable airline can help you feel safer and more comfortable.

Consider Domestic Flights: Bolivia's vast territory makes domestic flights a timesaving option for longdistance travel. Bolivia Airlines such as Bolivia Airlines

(BoA) and Amazon operate major city connections.

By local bus: Local buses are a great way to explore the city. In La Paz, El Alto and other parts of the city, micro buses and minibuses provide good and cheap transportation. Familiarize yourself with the routes and fare system.

Navigate Taxis Safely: Use official taxi services or ridesharing apps to ensure safety and fair pricing. Negotiate the fare before starting the journey, and be cautious of unmarked vehicles. In some cities, taxi meters are standard.

Be mindful of altitude: If you're heading to the highest destinations like La Paz or Potosi, expect altitude to affect your travel plans. Rest when you arrive, especially to get used to the lower altitudes. Coca tea is readily available and may help reduce symptoms of altitude sickness.

Rideshare Adventures: Rideshare vehicles (such as pickup trucks or shared taxis) are a form of urban travel. They provide a middle ground between bus and private transport, striking a balance between affordability and convenience.

Mountain Plan: Bolivia's mountainous terrain means the road is winding and sometimes difficult. If you are prone to the disease, consider taking precautions. Also be prepared for travel delays due to traffic, especially during the rainy season.

Road of Death Liability Information: If travel on the road of death near La Paz is not good, choose a renowned tour operator and a guide knowledgeable about safety. Make sure they provide the appropriate safety equipment and take care of your own driving.

Respect Local Driving Norms: If renting a vehicle, familiarize yourself with local driving norms. Road signs and driving conditions may vary, especially in rural areas. Exercise caution and be mindful of pedestrians and livestock on roads.

Utilize the Teleférico System: In La Paz, embrace the modern teleférico (cable car) system for stunning views of the city and efficient transportation. This is a unique and interesting way to explore the city's landscape.

Check transport regulations: If planning to travel by land, check visa and entry to departure and arrival countries. If you are driving, make sure your vehicle information is complete.

Be patient and flexible: Bolivia's transportation system will not adhere to rigid schedules. Be patient and flexible, especially when exploring remote areas. Delay may be part of the adventure. By incorporating these transportation tips into your travel plans, you can explore Bolivia's diverse landscapes with confidence and ease.

Whether you're soaring over the Andes by cable car or traveling across the country by bus, each mode of transportation adds a unique dimension to your Bolivian adventure. have a good journey! (Safe way!)

Cultural Etiquette

To have a good and rewarding experience in Bolivia, it is important to understand and respect the culture. Here are some important Bolivian traditions and customs that will help you interact with the locals:

Greetings and etiquette: It is customary to shake hands warmly when meeting someone for the first time. Your friends and family may greet you with hugs and kisses on the cheek. Address people by their first and last names as a sign of respect; Add "Don" for men and "Doña" for women.

Respect for personal space: Bolivians value personal space, especially in public. Keep a good distance when talking and do not stand too close to others. Respectful gestures and friendly behavior go a long way.

Timetable: The meeting schedule is generally relaxed, although time is generally welcome. Make things easier on time, especially in rural areas. However, it is recommended to arrive on time for business meetings and official events.

Meals and food sharing: Bolivians often share their meals for recreational purposes. If you are invited to someone's home, it is appropriate to bring a small gift such as candy or flowers. When eating, wait for the host to start eating and enjoy the meal before you start eating.

Traditional greetings in indigenous communities: In indigenous communities, traditional greetings may include the exchange of coca leaves. When coca leaves are offered, accepting them with both hands and giving them back is a sign of respect. Participate in these cultural exchanges with an open mind and curiosity.

Discussion topic: Bolivians are generally open and friendly. However, unless the conversation progresses in that direction, it is recommended to stay away from important topics such as politics and religion. Instead, talk about Bolivia's cultural interests, local traditions, and advantages.

Dress appropriately for specific occasions: When visiting religious sites or Aboriginal communities, dress in accordance with local customs. Women must cover their shoulders, men and women must remove their hats.

Learn simple expressions in Spanish and local languages: Although many Bolivians speak Spanish, especially in indigenous communities, learning some simple expressions in the local language can lead to respect for the culture. Quechua and Aymara are two indigenous languages.

Photography Rules: Always ask permission before taking photographs of people, especially in rural or Aboriginal areas. Some people may not like to be photographed, so please respect their wishes. It is necessary to ask vendors before occupying their markets during a market or festival.

Respect for indigenous culture: Bolivia is home to many indigenous communities, each with their own traditions and customs. Approach these communities with humility, obtain permission before entering sacred sites, and follow local guidelines.

Business Negotiation: Negotiation is a practice in business life. Think of this as a friendly conversation rather than an argument. Keep calm, smile and enjoy the conversation. Remember, a fair price benefits both you and the seller.

Show Your Gratitude: In Bolivian culture, it is important to show your gratitude. Whether it's at a restaurant or at someone's home, this is considered "gracias" (thank you) and we appreciate your hospitality.

By accepting these cultural practices you will develop good relationships and build relationships with the Bolivian people. Remember that openness, humility, and genuine interest in community leadership go a long way in creating cultural harmony. Thank you! (Very good relationship!)

Chapter 9. Photography Guide

Capturing Bolivia's Beauty

Bolivia's diverse landscapes, rich cultural tapestry, and vibrant traditions provide a photographer's paradise. Here are tips to help you capture the beauty of Bolivia through your lens:

Embrace the Golden Hours: Take advantage of the soft, warm light during sunrise and sunset, known as the golden hours. This magical light enhances Bolivia's landscapes, casting long shadows and creating a captivating atmosphere.

EXPLORE DIFFERENT LANDSCAPE: Bolivia is home to many landscapes, from the highaltitude Andes Mountains to the lush Amazon rainforest. Increase diversity by exploring different fields, each with their own unique perspective.

Highlighting Indigenous Culture: Highlighting the beautiful traditions and beautiful clothing of Bolivia's indigenous communities. Attend local festivals, markets and celebrations to capture the essence of this rich cultural experience.

Utilize WideAngle Lenses: Wideangle lenses are ideal for capturing the expansive vistas of Bolivia's landscapes. Whether photographing the vastness of Salar de Uyuni or the towering peaks of the Andes, wide angles help convey the grandeur of the scenery.

Experiment with Reflections: During the rainy season, Salar de Uyuni transforms into a giant mirror. Try your imagination to create beautiful, surreal images. Use your imagination to make it look like you're shooting the sky below you.

Capturing Street Life: Bolivia's cities and markets are full of street life. Candid shots of people going about their daily activities, bustling markets and colorful streetscapes give us a glimpse into the heart of the country.

Composition: Use natural products to enhance your learning. Whether it's the arches of Sucre's colonial architecture or the lush foliage of the Amazon, framing will add depth and visual interest to your photos.

View Details: Shows beautiful details of Bolivia's cultural artifacts, traditional clothing, and architectural elements. These relationships provide detailed information and tell beautiful business and leadership stories.

Chasing impressive skies: Bolivia's highaltitude landscape can form huge clouds. Add dynamic skies to your compositions to add mood and dimension to your photos.

Respect for Cultural Sensitivity: When photographing people, especially in Aboriginal communities, seek their permission and respect their views if they refuse. Have a friendly chat to create conversation before taking photos.

Arresting festivals and celebrations: Bolivia's festivals, such as the Oruro Carnival or the Gran Poder parade in La Paz, are full of energy and visual beauty. Plan your visit around these events to capture the energy, color and culture of the show.

Beyond the famous places: While photographing iconic places like Salar de Uyuni is a must, don't ignore the beauty of unknown places. Explore pristine regions, discover hidden gems and capture Bolivia's hidden treasures.

Whether you are an amateur photographer or a professional, Bolivia offers the perfect opportunity to capture beautiful moments. Let the country's beauty and rich culture inspire your imagination; You will be rewarded with a collection of photographs that tell the fascinating story of Bolivia. Happy photography! (Happy photo!)

Best Photo Spots

Bolivia's diverse locations delight photographers. Here are some of the best photo spots that showcase the beauty of the country:

Salar de Uyuni: Salar de Uyuni, the world's largest salt flat, offers a completely different view, creating a beautiful view during the dry season. Vast white spaces and spectacular views make this a mustvisit destination.

Isla Incahuasi: Located in the heart of the Salar de Uyuni, Isla Incahuasi is a rocky island covered with giant cacti. Keep the contrast of the cactus with a solid background for a beautiful photo.

Laguna Colorada: Eduardo Avaloa Located in the Andes Fauna National Reserve, this pink lake is a flamingowatching paradise. The sparkling lake and surrounding mountains create a surreal, picturesque landscape.

Palacio Quemado (Presidential Palace) La Paz: The ornate Presidential Palace in La Paz, with its historic architecture and vibrant surroundings, provides an excellent opportunity for capturing the city's cultural and political significance.

Yungas Road (Death Road): Brave the infamous Death Road on a mountain bike for thrilling action shots and breathtaking views. The winding road and lush landscapes offer a unique perspective of Bolivia's natural beauty.

Mirador Killi Killi La Paz: This viewpoint in La Paz offers spectacular views of the city and surrounding mountains. Visit at sunset to catch the city lights of the Andes.

Tiahuanaco Archaeological Site: Explore the ruins of ancient Tiahuanaco, capturing the complexity of preColumbian architecture and the spiritual significance of the archaeological site.

Rooftop Views of Potosi: Climb to the top of the roof of a colonial house in Potosi for a panoramic view of the city and the historic Cerro Rico mountain, which played an important role in Bolivian history.

Laguna Verde: Located at the base of the Licancabur Volcano, Laguna Verde is fascinating with its turquoise waters. The views of the surrounding peak make this an attractive photo spot.

Plaza Murillo La Paz: The central square in La Paz, surrounded by landmarks like the Cathedral and the Presidential Palace, provides opportunities for street photography and capturing the vibrant atmosphere of the city.

Uyuni Train Cemetery: This eerie and fascinating graveyard of abandoned trains near Uyuni offers a unique backdrop for creative and atmospheric photography.

Sucre's Historic District: Wander through the colonial streets of Sucre, a UNESCO World Heritage site. Capture the wellpreserved architecture and the timeless charm of Bolivia's constitutional capital. From the stark beauty of the salt flats to the historical richness of Bolivia's cities, each photo spot presents a unique opportunity to capture the essence of this South American gem.

Whether you're drawn to natural wonders or cultural landmarks, Bolivia offers a visual playground for photographers. ¡Buenas fotos! (Happy shooting!)

Editing and Sharing Tips

Once you've captured the beauty of Bolivia through your lens, enhance and share your memories with editing and sharing instructions:

Organize your shots: Organize photos into folders by location, subject or event before editing. This makes the repair process more efficient.

Choose the right editing software: Choose a photo editing tool that suits your skill level and preferences. Adobe Lightroom and Photoshop are powerful options; Applications such as Snapseed and VSCO offer users mobile editing.

Pay attention to the color: Bolivia's landscape has beautiful colors. Adjust saturation and vibrancy to improve tone, but be careful not to overdo it. Strive for the balance of truth.

Adjust contrast and accuracy: Alignment and accuracy are adjusted to bring out details in shadows and highlights. This is essential to capture the different lights of Bolivia, from the bright salt to the shadowy area.

Experimenting with filters and presets: Explore filters and presets to give your photos a special touch. Experiment with different styles, but make sure your edits match the mood and location of each shot.

Crop and Straighten: Crop your photos to improve composition and eliminate distractions. Enhance the horizon for a beautiful view, especially in landscape photos.

Be Authentic: While editing can improve your image, try to keep it authentic to the scene you shot. Avoid excessive retouching that could alter Bolivia's beauty.

Tell a story with a sequence: If you have photos from a special place or event, consider creating a sequence to tell the story people see This is especially effective when sharing on social media or photo albums.

Add watermarks strategically: If you choose to add watermarks to your photos, do so strategically and wisely. Place the watermark in a corner where it will not interfere with the main content.

Resize for different platforms: Resize the image according to your assigned platform. For example, Instagram has a custom aspect ratio. Adjust your photos accordingly.

Write a Personal Statement: Create a coherent sentence that summarizes or tells an interesting story about your image. Adding a personal touch can improve viewers' connection to your photos.

Choose a shared platform: Choose a platform that suits your goals. Instagram is a great platform for telling visual stories, while platforms like Flickr or SmugMug allow for detailed photos. Share your experiences in travel forums and communities and connect with other likeminded people.

BONUS TIP:

Engage with your audience: Respond to comments and messages when sharing Bolivia images. Engaging with your audience creates a sense of community, allowing you to share your insights and experiences. By connecting updates and sharing tips you can make your Bolivian adventure a beautiful and rewarding experience.

Whether you create a digital photo album, share on social media, or curate a collection, your photos can showcase the unique beauty of this South American gem. Enjoy sharing! (Happy sharing!)

Chapter 10. Conclusion

Recap of Highlights

Begin a virtual journey and let's review the highlights of your adventure in Bolivia, the land of diversity and beauty:

View Bolivia Culture: From the traditional shops of La Paz to the ancient ruins of Tiahuanaco, you will be immersed in the rich cultural fabric of Bolivia. The warm welcome, the bright colors of Andean costumes and the enchanting performances of indigenous troupes leave an indelible mark.

His Majesty Salar de Uyuni: Standing on the great Salar de Uyuni, the largest salt flat in the world, you see a surreal beauty that seems to reach its end. The mirror effect in summer and the unique topography of Incahuasi make this impression a photo paradise.

Andes and Colorado Lakes: Travel through the Andes and marvel at red, brown and green landscapes. Surrounded by majestic peaks and with flamingofilled waters, the stunning Lake Colorado showcases the raw beauty of Bolivia's highlands.

Colonial Charm of Sucre and Potosi: Explore the historical sites of Sucre and Potosi and step back into Bolivia's colonial days. The cobblestone streets, ornate churches and rooftop views of Rico in Potosi offer a glimpse into the country's colonial past and architectural splendor.

Thrill of Death: Beat death's death on a mountain bike on the way back from Yongas area. The adrenaline rush combined with breathtaking views turns this exciting adventure into an unforgettable experience.

Lakes and Volcanoes: Located at the base of the Licancabur Volcano, Laguna Verde showcases Bolivia's spectacular alpine lake. The contrast between the turquoise water and the mountain is beautiful.

Lifestyle and Workstyle: Capture the lifestyle and bustling work of Bolivian villages, see the daily rhythms of the country. From the big works in La Paz to the fascinating witch market, these events show the heart and culture of Bolivian cities.

Aboriginal Experience: You come into contact with Aboriginal communities and learn about their customs and traditions. From exchanging coca leaves to colorful celebrations, these interactions provide a deeper understanding of Bolivia's diverse culture.

Architectural Marvels and Natural Wonders: Enjoy the finest architecture, such as the La Paz Presidential Palace and the ancient ruins of Tiahuanaco, while balancing the experience between cultural exploration and Bolivia's nature.

Taste of Bolivia Food Tour: Enjoy Bolivian cuisine while tasting signature dishes such as salteñas, site de pollo and cuñapé. Every bite becomes a culinary discovery that adds flavor to your trip.

Your trip to Bolivia is a rich experience that includes ancient traditions as well as modern adventure, curiosity and culture. While you think about these important points, maybe you can remember the beauties of Bolivia like a beautiful record in your travel history. ¡ How to install Aventura! (Until the next adventure!)

Inspiring Future Travelers

For those who dream of distant beaches and seek adventure along the way, Bolivia stands out with its unique beauty and richness. This is an invitation to encourage future travelers to begin their journey of discovery:

Open the door to discovery: Bolivia, the land where the spirit of fun is in the air, invites you to open the door to discovery. Trade beyond the obvious and embrace the thrill of exploring a landscape beyond your imagination.

TAPESTAL OF CULTURAL DIVERSITY: Immerse yourself in the diversity of Bolivia. From the traditional markets of La Paz to the ancient culture of Uruchipaya, each encounter reveals a unique symbol of the country's rich cultural mosaic.

Song of the Siren of Salar de Uyuni: Answer to the song of the Siren of Salar de Uyuni, the ethereal salt flat mirror in the sky. Finally walk, the line between sky and ground disappears, leaving you suspended in the dream.

Dance the Road of Death: Dance the legendary Road of Death, where the breathtaking view that unfolds at every turn is matched by the excitement of the centers. An adrenalinefilled journey that meets the beauty of Bolivia's Yungas region.

Whispers of Ancient Ruins: Hear the whispers of the ancient ruins of Tiahuanaco, where stones tell the story of preColumbian civilization. Admire other temples and statues that speak of the greatness of Bolivian history.

A Bolivianflavored journey: Embark on a Bolivianflavored culinary journey. From delicious Salteñas to comforting hot API, each dish is an epiphany that invites you to taste the essence of Bolivian cuisine.

High Altitude Lakes and Volcanoes:
Climb to high altitude lakes like Lake Colorado and witness the action. Feel the fresh mountain air as you stand in the shadow of the mighty volcano, surrounded by soulstirring landscapes.

Culturally Vibrant Market: Enter a market that is on the pulse of Bolivian culture. Be mesmerized by the bright colors of fabrics and the sounds of daily life in the markets of La Paz. Witches Market is a mysterious world that invites you to discover its secrets.

Cultural Exchange with Aboriginal Communities: Cultural exchange with Aboriginal communities where traditions are integrated into daily life. There is a warm bond created by sharing and exchanging coca leaves.

Preservation of the colonial city's heritage: Walk along the cobblestone streets of Sucre and Potosi, where the pavements are a testament to Bolivia's historical heritage. These cities are like living canvases, inviting you to paint your memories of unforgettable moments.

Natural Drama Around Every Corner: Witness the natural drama around every corner of Bolivia, from the turquoise waters of Laguna Verde to the lush Amazon rainforest. This is a country where the landscape changes seamlessly, evoking a sense of wonder at every turn.

Invitation: Bolivia has an invitation for future travelers; It invites you to the forest reaching to the sky, a strong economy and a deep culture. Answer the call and prepare to uncover a neverbeforeseen perspective of Bolivia.

Bolivia awaits those who dare to dream; a canvas of inspiration that brings new discoveries with every step. The journey is calling and unprecedented miracles are about to unfold. ¡ How to install Aventura! (Until the next adventure!)

Printed in Great Britain
by Amazon